TEACHING
—IN THE—
SPIRIT

SECOND EDITION

DENZIL R. MILLER

TEACHING
—IN THE—
SPIRIT

DENZIL R. MILLER

PneumaLife Publications
Springfield, MO, USA

Second Edition, Published in 2013 by PnrumaLife Publications, Springfield, MO, USA

Teaching in the Spirit. Copyright © 2009 by Denzil R. Miller. All rights reserved. No part of this book may be reproduced, stored in a retrieval system, or transmitted in any form or by any means—electronic, mechanical, photocopy, recording, or otherwise—without prior written permission of the copyright owner, except brief quotations used in connection with reviews in magazines or newspapers.

Formerly published as *The Holy Spirit and Teaching: A Pentecostal Perspective,* © 1995 Denny Miller. Updated and Revised as *Teaching in the Spirit,* 2009. Second Edition 2013

All scripture quotations, unless otherwise noted, are taken from the HOLY BIBLE, NEW INTERNATIONAL VERSION, copyright 1973, 1978, 1984 by the International Bible Society. All rights reserved.

Libraries of Congress Cataloging-in-Publication Data
Miller, Denzil R., 1946–
Teaching in the Spirit
Denzil R. Miller

ISBN: 978-0-9911332-1-5

1. Teaching—Pentecostal 2. Biblical teaching— 3. Biblical studies—Holy Spirit

Printed in the United States of America

CONTENTS

Introduction 1

1   The Holy Spirit in the Content of
New Testament Teaching 7

2   The Holy Spirit in the Content of Contemporary
Pentecostal Teaching 25

3   The Holy Spirit in the Context of
Pentecostal Teaching 41

4   The Holy Spirit in the Presentation of
Pentecostal Teaching 55

Bibliography 63

Other Books by the Author 65

INTRODUCTION

More than a decade ago, in a landmark 1994 statistical report of the Assemblies of God, USA, a startling finding was announced. In a national survey, it was revealed that for the first time in its eighty-year history, more than half of the church's U.S. membership had not been baptized in the Holy Spirit as were the believers on the Day of Pentecost (Acts 1:8; 2:4). Since that time the percentage of members baptized in the Spirit has continued in a steady decline.

That same year, in its quarterly periodical, *Harvest Messenger* (First Quarter, 1994), the Africa Harvest Projects and Coordinating Office (now Africa Harvest Ministries), a subsidiary of the U.S. Assemblies of God World Missions, Africa Office, made an even more startling announcement concerning their African churches. The report revealed that although the Assemblies of God (AG) in Africa were indeed experiencing dramatic growth across the continent, they were, at the same time, becoming less and less Pentecostal, at least *experientially*. It was reported that only about 20 percent of their constituency was baptized in the Holy Spirit. By the year 2000 the percentage has decreased to 17 percent. If that figure holds true today, its means that, of their current 15 million constituents in the Assemblies of God in Africa only 2.5 million have been baptized in the Spirit, leaving 12.5 million who have not experienced the Pentecostal baptism. Although I have not done research on other fields in the world, anecdotal evidence seems to indicate that the same is true for the Assemblies of God worldwide.

Introduction

The Assemblies of God stand at a crossroads. It is a crossroads in that area of Pentecostal experience and practice. Country by country the movement's more than 200 filial national churches must decide for themselves whether they want to continue as Spirit-empowered missionary movements, or to become, as one missionary leader described them, merely fellowships of "enthusiastic Evangelicals."

As many are realizing, the time has come for the alarm to be clearly and repeatedly sounded. If the church does not take immediate and dramatic steps to remedy this disturbing trend, the world's largest Pentecostal fellowship is in real danger of sacrificing our evangelistic and missionary impetus promised by Jesus (Acts 1:8) and exemplified by the Assemblies of God since its inception in 1914. If the movement does not experience a worldwide revival of Pentecost, with tens of millions of its members being baptized in the Spirit, it could, in this generation, cease to be a truly Pentecostal church. By that, I mean a church that is Pentecostal, not in doctrine only, but in experience and practice.

If only a minority of our constituency is truly filled with the Spirit and focused on the Great Commission of Christ, then we must ask the question, "Why?" We ask the question, not to ascribe blame, but to seek solutions. What have we failed to do that we must now begin to do? Certainly, there is cause for alarm—and immediate action. The issue is not how many people we can get to speak tongues and thus qualify as a "Pentecostal" church. The issue is the eternal destiny of millions of lost souls. If the Assemblies of God around the world will experience a new Pentecostal dynamic, and thus begin to move in the power of the Spirit with biblical signs following, this will result in literally millions of souls being swept into the church—and ultimately into heaven—in the remaining years before Christ returns. But if the church fails in this all important area, millions will be eternally lost.

Introduction

While observing this not-too-encouraging trend, I have, at the same time, observed another more encouraging circumstance in our churches, at least on the continent of Africa, where I have ministered for the past sixteen years. Even though the great majority of our members are not presently baptized in the Spirit, I have observed that they are ready and eager to be filled. Like the household of Cornelius, they eagerly await the message of Pentecost (Acts 10:24-25). During my years in Africa I have traveled throughout the continent preaching and teaching the message of the baptism in the Holy Spirit. In Malawi alone, where I lived from 1993 through 2007, I preached in more than 300 Assemblies of God churches. Wherever I traveled, I have found the people enthusiastically receptive to the Pentecostal message. Typically, after I have preached, well over half of the congregation joyfully responded, presenting themselves to be filled with the Spirit. And when we have prayed with them, most are immediately filled with the Spirit. I have seen it happen again and again in churches throughout Africa.[1] I have also seen this same enthusiasm in several of our Bible schools throughout the region. The time is ripe for a great Pentecostal awakening in our churches. I pray that we don't miss this God's given opportunity.

The question that we as Pentecostal leaders, pastors, missionaries, and educators must ask ourselves is, "Do we really want to remain a truly Pentecostal church?" If we fail to address this critical issue—with the vast majority of our worldwide constituencies not filled with the Spirit, including, I am

---

[1] During my years in Africa it has been my privilege to conduct Holy Spirit emphases in Malawi, Kenya, Tanzania, Rwanda, Ethiopia, Sudan, Mauritius, Madagascar, South Africa, Zambia, Zimbabwe, Namibia, Botswana, Gabon, Equatorial Guinea, Congo, the Democratic Republic of Congo, Nigeria, Togo, Mali, Chad, Togo, Benin, Ghana, Burkina Faso, and Ivory Coast.

discovering, in some countries, a significant percentage of our pastors—the tide in our churches will soon turn against Pentecost, and the day will be lost. This decade will decide. What we do today will determine our future as a movement.

I believe that, more than anyone else, the teachers in our Bible schools hold the key to the future of the movement. This book is written specifically for these Pentecostal educators. The occasion for the original presentation of the lessons that have become the core of this book was a regional conference of Assemblies of God Bible school teachers sponsored by the African Theological Training Services (now Africa's Hope). The conference was held in Dodoma, Tanzania, in November of 1995. I was given the assignment to teach on the topic "Teaching and the Holy Spirit." As I began to pray about this matter, I sensed the Holy Spirit directing me to narrow my topic to "The Holy Spirit and the Pentecostal Bible School Teacher." I decided that in my sessions I would speak directly to Pentecostal teachers of Pentecostal preachers. These lessons became a call for a Pentecostal model of Bible teaching. The lessons were so well received that several teachers asked for my notes, and I was asked by the late Dr. John York to pen this book.

There is a popular American comedian who has elicited many laughs from his audiences by claiming that he "don't get no respect!" I suppose that is how many teachers in our Pentecostal Bible schools feel also. It seems that teachers are often the least honored of all the ministry gifts. This is especially true in our Pentecostal movement. I suppose this is because of our Pentecostal love for the supernatural and spectacular. Apostles, prophets, evangelists, and even pastors, seem better able to provide such sensational performances than our teachers.

And yet, we teachers certainly must shoulder our part of the blame for this lack of enthusiasm concerning our ministries. In his

Introduction

book *Spiritual Gifts in the Work of the Ministry Today*, pioneer Pentecostal preacher and educator, Donald Gee, wrote,

> It has to be ruefully admitted that teachers, as such, often undermined their own acceptance because they brought over into the Pentecostal Revival the methods they had used in their former denominational churches.[2]

This indictment, we must honestly admit, is all too true.

The purpose of this book is to help rectify this very problem. Its purpose is to present a truly New Testament, and thus truly Pentecostal, model for teaching. In my more than 25 years of Pentecostal ministry as a pastor and teacher, I cannot say that I have ever been presented with such a model for teaching. Although, I must admit upon reflection, that some of my teachers, to varying degrees, have approached this model in practice.

In this book I will approach the subject of the work of the Holy Spirit in teaching from three directions. In Chapters 1 and 2, I will deal with "The Holy-Spirit in the *Content* of Pentecostal Teaching." In Chapter 3, I will discuss, "The Holy Spirit in the *Context* of Pentecostal Teaching." And finally, in Chapter 4, I will explore, "The Holy Spirit in the *Presentation* of Pentecostal Teaching." It is my sincere desire that as a result of this book the teachers in our Bible schools throughout Africa (and the world) will become truly Pentecostal in their teaching, thus producing the army of genuinely Pentecostal preachers we will need to evangelize Africa and beyond.

---

[2] Donald Gee, *The Gifts of the Spirit in the Working of the Ministry Today,* (Springfield, MO: Gospel Publishing House, 1963), 2.

Introduction

— CHAPTER 1 —

THE HOLY SPIRIT IN THE CONTENT OF NEW TESTAMENT TEACHING

It should go without saying that every Pentecostal pastor must have a comprehensive understanding of what the Bible says about the Holy Spirit. In his locality he must be seen as the "resident expert" in things concerning the Spirit of God. His understanding of the subject must be both comprehensive and biblically sound. Such a thorough understanding will help him in several areas of his spiritual ministry. First, this sound biblical understanding will serve as the foundation for all of his ministry in the Spirit. Because of this understanding, he will be able to move with poise and confidence as he ministers under the anointing of the Spirit of God.

In addition, this solid biblical foundation will protect him from doctrinal error. His feet will be firmly planted in the clear teaching of Scripture on the subject. Just as important, it will equip him to shield his congregation from the strange winds of doctrine that so often blow through the Pentecostal/charismatic community (Eph.4: 14).

Yet another benefit of this solid biblical foundation will be that the minister will be helped in defending his doctrinal position as a Pentecostal leader. In the area of Pentecostal doctrine and practice he will "always be prepared to give an answer to everyone who asks [him] to give the reason for the hope that [he has]" (1 Pet. 3:15).

A thorough understanding of the Spirit and His work will also help the Pentecostal minister reach out to others with the message of Pentecost. Through his ministry their lives can be enriched and their witnesses to the world enhanced as they come into a fuller personal knowledge of the Spirit of God.

How tragic it is when people, hungry for a deeper relationship with God, come to the Pentecostal pastor only to find him ill-equipped to help them. Instead of giving them clear biblical direction, he gives them a confusing jumble of inconsistencies and underdeveloped ideas. I relate a personal experience as an illustration of this. After graduating from Bible college in 1969, I was called to serve as pastor of a small rural church in southeast Colorado. Soon after arriving, I learned from some of the local non-Pentecostal pastors of an experience they had had with my pastoral predecessor. Some of these pastors had become interested in the Pentecostal baptism, and had called a meeting, requesting that my predecessor, the pastor of the local Assemblies of God church, come and explain to them the baptism in the Holy Spirit.

Upon arriving at the meeting, this pastor—at least according to the report I received—rather than guide them into the biblical experience they sought, began to extol the glories of the King James Version of the Bible, while at the same time condemning the particular translation of the Bible these men were accustomed to using. He then went on to explain to them how the "Holy Ghost" in his Bible was not the same thing as the "Holy Spirit" in their more "liberal" Bibles. He, of course, soon lost his audience. He also lost his God-given opportunity to help some hungry seekers after the Spirit of God. What a tragedy! I can only wonder how many other hungry seekers have been disillusioned by zealous, how be it, ill-qualified Pentecostal ministers.

It is the responsibility of the Pentecostal Bible school teacher to see that his students are fully qualified to perform their God-given duties. He must see that they possess a clear and complete understanding of the person and work of the Holy Spirit. We as Pentecostal teachers must commit ourselves to teaching clearly, comprehensively, and convincingly, about the Holy Spirit and His work. We must remember that such teaching is not only Pentecostal; it is indeed biblical. We need look no further than the Master Teacher of the ages, Jesus Christ Himself, to confirm this fact.

THE HOLY SPIRIT IN THE CONTENT OF JESUS' TEACHING

The teaching of Jesus is alive with instruction about the Holy Spirit. He taught often on the subject of the Spirit and His work. For illustrative purposes I have chosen six representative examples from the many instances that Jesus taught on the Holy Spirit.

Everyone Who Asks Receives

Our first example of Jesus' teaching about the Holy Spirit is found in Luke 11:5-13. Here, in the context of His teaching His disciples about prayer, Jesus explains to them how they may be filled with the Holy Spirit. He teaches them several things. He instructs them in the vital importance of being filled with the Spirit by encouraging them to keep on asking, keep on seeking, and keep on knocking. If they will do this, then God will keep on filling them with His Spirit (v. 9). He informs them of the wonderful availability of the Holy Spirit, as He tells them that "everyone who asks receives" (v. 10). And He allays their fears of a false or demonic baptism by teaching them that their Heavenly Father will give them exactly what they ask for—the Holy Spirit—and nothing else (vv. 11-13).

That Which is Born of Spirit is Spirit

A second example of the Holy Spirit in the content of Jesus' teaching is found in John 3. There He teaches another teacher about the Holy Spirit. He instructs the Jewish rabbi, Nicodemus, concerning the work of the Holy Spirit in regeneration. Jesus straightforwardly teaches this man about the absolute necessity of a spiritual rebirth before one can *enter,* or for that matter, even *see* the kingdom of God (vv. 3, 7). He teaches Nicodemus that only "Spirit gives birth to spirit" (v. 6). Then, in verse eight, Jesus gives Nicodemus a short, yet penetrating, teaching on the nature and work of the Holy Spirit. He figuratively speaks of the sovereign will of the Holy Spirit ("the wind blows wherever it pleases"); He hints at the visible results of the Spirit's work in the lives of men ("you hear its sound"); and He alludes to both the incomprehensible origin ("but cannot tell where it comes from"); and the mysterious destiny of the Spirit ("or where it is going"). Oh, the profound depth of this teaching of Jesus about the Holy Spirit!

If I by the Spirit of God Drive out Demons

A third example of Jesus teaching on the Holy Spirit is found in Matthew 12 where the people brought to Jesus a demonized man who was both blind and mute. Jesus cast out the demon, thus healing the man of both infirmities. The people were amazed and wondered if Jesus could be the promised Jewish Messiah. The religious leaders, however, accused him of casting out demons by the power of Beelzebub, the prince of the demons (vv. 24). Jesus used this occasion to teach two essential lessons concerning the Holy Spirit.

First, He taught them that it is through the Spirit of God that we drive out demons, and thus helping to advance God's kingdom in the world (v. 28). He expands on this subject in the next verse, when He teaches that it is through the same power of the Spirit that we can "bind the strong man" and "plunder his goods." In other words, we, through the Holy Spirit, have been given the power to bind demonic powers, and thus liberate those people who live under their evil domination.

Jesus then uses the same incident as an occasion to teach concerning the blasphemy of the Holy Spirit. He teaches them that, although blasphemy against the Son of Man can be forgiven, "anyone who speaks against Holy Spirit will not be forgiven, either in this age or the age to come" (v. 32).

Rivers of Living Water
Another example of Jesus teaching about the Holy Spirit is found in John 7. Tradition tells us that at a certain point during the last day of the week-long Feast of the Tabernacles, a procession of Jewish priests would enter the temple court with containers of water drawn from the Pool of Siloam. In the presence of all the people they would ceremoniously pour out the water as a reminder of how God had miraculously provided water when their fore bearers had thirsted in the wilderness. Jesus used this occasion to teach a magnificent lesson about the Holy Spirit. He cried out, "If anyone is thirsty, let him come unto me and drink. Whoever believes in me, as the Scripture has said, streams of living water will flow from within him" (vv. 37-38). John interprets Jesus' teaching: "By this he meant the Spirit, whom those who believed in him were later to receive. Up to that time the Spirit had not been given, since Jesus had not yet been glorified" (v. 39). Jesus thus

taught about how the same Holy Spirit would both quench our spiritual thirsts (4:10-14), and flow from us to be a blessing to others.

Another Counselor

A fifth example of Jesus' extensive teaching on the Holy Spirit is found in John 14-16. In chapter 14 He makes an amazing—almost breathtaking—promise. He says that those who believe in Him will do the same works that they had seen Him do. Even more, they will do even greater works than He (v. 12). Jesus is, no doubt, speaking of works of greater quantity, rather than greater quality. One writer contends that this greater work is the fulfillment of Jesus' Great Commission to preach the gospel to every creature. Be that as it may, Jesus then tells why they will be able to do these greater works when He says, it is "because I am going to the Father." Jesus explains that His going to the Father will result in His sending the Holy Spirit (15:26, 16:7; cf. Acts 2:32-33). The promise is that every believer can be filled with the same Holy Spirit who filled and empowered Him during his earthly ministry, thus enabling them to do the same works He did.

In the same chapter, Jesus expands on the theme of the coming of the Holy Spirit (14:15-18). He tells His disciples that He would ask the Father and He will give them "another Counselor" to be with them forever. He identifies this other Counselor as "the Spirit of truth" (v. 17). He then explains to them that He would not abandon them as orphans, but He would come to them in the person of the Holy Spirit. Later, He tells them that the Holy Spirit will take His place as their Teacher: "But the Counselor, the Holy Spirit, ... will teach you all things and will remind you of everything I have said to you" (v. 26).

In chapter 16 Jesus teaches concerning, what one commentator has called "the office work of the Spirit." He says that, when the Holy Spirit comes, He will "convict the world of guilt in regard to sin and righteousness and judgement" (v. 8). In other words, a principal work of the Holy Spirit will be that of convincing and convicting men concerning the truth of the message of the gospel of Jesus Christ.

You Will Receive Power

A final example of Jesus' teaching about the Holy Spirit is found in Acts 1. This is Jesus' last recorded "class session" with His disciples before leaving them and ascending into heaven. During this final session with His disciples Jesus could have taught about many important matters. He chose, however, to teach them one final lesson on the Holy Spirit. Luke writes that, on that occasion, He "gave instructions through the Holy Spirit to the apostles he had chosen," and "spoke about the kingdom of God" (vv. 2-3). What were these instructions, and what were these things concerning the kingdom of God that He taught about? We have the answer to these questions, at least in part, in the command He immediately gave to His disciples:

> Do not leave Jerusalem, but wait for the gift my Father promised, which you have heard me speak about. For John baptized with water, but in a few days you will be baptized with the Holy Spirit. (vv. 4-5)

Then, in verse 8, He tells them the purpose of this baptism in the Holy Spirit. Its purpose was that they might receive power to proclaim His gospel to the "ends of the earth" (v. 8).

The Lesson of His Life

It also deserves mention that, not only did Jesus teach orally about the Holy Spirit, His entire life was a profound lesson on how to walk, live, and minister in the power and anointing of the Holy Spirit.

THE HOLY SPIRIT IN THE CONTENT OF THE BELIEVERS' TEACHING IN THE BOOK OF ACTS

Following the example of Jesus, the early church preached and taught frequently on the subject of the Holy Spirit. If we define teaching as the transfer of new truth from one who is more knowledgeable to one who is less knowledgeable, then most, if not all, of the sermons in Acts contain teaching as well as proclamation.

Peter's Pentecost Sermon

One example is what is commonly known as Peter's Pentecost "sermon" delivered in Jerusalem on the Day of Pentecost. Closer investigation reveals that this sermon was not a sermon at all, at least in the traditional sense. It was more properly a prophetic utterance. Just as the 120, under the inspiration of the Holy Spirit, spoke in unlearned languages, now Peter utters forth a prophetic message from God in the common language.[3]

---

[3] I say this because of the word Luke uses when he writes that Peter "raised his voice and *addressed* the crowd" (v. 14). The word here translated "addressed" is taken from the Greek verb *apephthenxato*, which literally means to "utter forth." It is the same verb that Luke used ("*began* to speak") to describe how the 120 received the ability to speak in tongues (2:4).

It was in the context of this prophetic message that Peter began to give the church's first teaching on the Holy Spirit.[4] In this message Peter teaches several things about the Holy Spirit:

1. The outpouring of the Holy Spirit that the crowd was witnessing was a fulfillment of a prophecy made by Joel (vv. 17-21).
2. This outpouring was for all people, and it would be accompanied by supernatural manifestations such as visions and prophecies (vv. 17-18).
3. It was the exalted Christ who had received authority from the Father to pour out the Holy Spirit (v. 33).
4. Those who would repent and be baptized in Jesus' name were candidates to receive the Holy Spirit (vv. 38-39).
5. This gift of the Holy Spirit was for everyone of every age whom God would call (v. 39).

Thus, the first recorded lesson taught by the New Testament church was filled with teaching about the work of the Holy Spirit.

The Household of Cornelius

Another example of teaching on the subject of the Holy Spirit is the sermon of Peter at the house of Cornelius in the coastal town of Caesarea (Acts 10). It was through a Spirit-inspired vision, and then a revelatory word spoken by the Spirit of God, that Peter was directed to go to Caesarea to speak to the Roman centurion, Cornelius, and his household (vv. 9-22). Upon arriving, Peter, as was his custom, declared the gospel unto them. He also taught concerning the work of the Holy Spirit in Jesus' life:

---

[4] And who says that teaching cannot contain a prophetic element, or that prophecy cannot contain an element of teaching? I will have more to say about this later in this study.

How God anointed Jesus of Nazareth with the Holy Spirit and power, and how he went around doing good and healing all who were under the power of the devil, because God was with him. (v. 38)

Since we believe that the sermons of the book of Acts are often abbreviated forms of longer sermons, we understand that a brief mention can often suggest that much more was spoken on that particular subject. Whether this is true in this instance, the effect of Peter's teaching concerning the Holy Spirit was both immediate and dramatic, for the Bible says that "while Peter was still speaking these words, the Holy Spirit came on all who heard the message " (v. 44). True to apostolic form, in his very first teaching to these people, Peter instructs them concerning the person and work of the Spirit of God.

Aquila and Priscilla Teach Apollos

The ministry of Priscilla and Aquila to Apollos is yet another possible example of teaching on the subject of the Holy Spirit in Acts. In Acts 18:24-25 Luke gives to us a thumbnail sketch of this mighty preacher named Apollos: He was an Alexandrian Jew, an eloquent speaker, and mighty in the Scriptures. Further, he possessed an accurate knowledge of the things of Christ and a burning zeal for the work of the Lord. The only baptism he knew, however, was the baptism of John. After hearing him preach in the synagogue of Ephesus, Aquila and Priscilla took him aside and explained to him the ways of God more accurately (v. 26).

Although we cannot be dogmatic at this point, the context of this passage, particularly the parallel situation in 19:1-6, where Paul deals with twelve other disciples in Ephesus who were in the same position as Apollos, implies that the husband/wife team taught Apollos about the work of the Spirit in his life. The effectiveness of his subsequent ministry seems to indicate that he received the gift of the Holy Spirit (vv. 27-28).

Paul in Ephesus

A final example of teaching about the Holy Spirit in Acts is Paul's dealing with the twelve disciples in Ephesus (19:1-7). Upon arriving in the city, he encountered twelve men. He immediately began to teach them about the necessity of one's being filled with the Holy Spirit. He asked them, "Did you receive the Holy Spirit when you believed?" Paul was enquiring into their readiness to participate in his mission of reaching all of Asia Minor with the gospel (v. 10). Although the text does not say, Paul's teaching could have continued along this vein for some time.

Then, having finished his teaching, Paul dealt with their personal experience, as do all effective teachers. After having them baptized in water, he laid his hands on them and "the Holy Spirit came on them, and they spoke with tongues and prophesied" (v. 6).

From these fives examples in the book of Acts we can draw certain conclusions concerning the Holy Spirit in the content of the early church's teaching. First, we can conclude that the message of the baptism in the Holy Spirit was a definite priority in apostolic preaching and teaching. In almost every occasion the subject was brought up in the very first message to any group where the gospel was presented. There was no hesitancy at all on the part of the apostles to present the message of the gift of the Holy Spirit to the multitudes in their initial evangelistic encounter.

Second, we conclude that the primitive church had much to say about the person and work of the Spirit. Teaching about the Holy Spirit pervades the book of Acts. I believe that we as Pentecostal teachers today should take our cue from these first century believers. Our teaching ministry should also be filled with content about the Holy Spirit.

THE HOLY SPIRIT IN THE CONTENT OF PAUL'S EPISTLES

Not only do we find much teaching about the Holy Spirit in the Gospels and Acts, we also discover that the letters of Paul are replete with teaching about the Holy Spirit. According to Gordon D. Fee, "The word 'spirit' *(pneuma)* occurs 145 times in the thirteen letters [of Paul], the vast majority of which unambiguously refer to the Holy Spirit..."[5] A thoughtful rereading of Paul's epistles reveals that teaching about the Holy Spirit pops up everywhere, even in the most unexpected places. When Paul is discussing what might at first appear to be an unrelated topic such as justification by faith or the second coming of Christ, the subject of the Holy Spirit appears.

Reread Paul's letters with a highlighter in hand. Every time you see the Holy Spirit or His work mentioned, highlight that passage. You will be amazed at how many times you use your highlighter. I have done this very thing in one of my Bibles. It is filled with passages highlighted in bright orange. When teaching on this subject I often lift this Bible and show it to my listeners. As I do, I page through the letters of Paul showing them the many reverences he makes to the person and work of the Holy Spirit.

In order to illustrate this point more clearly let's imagine that the letters of Paul are oral sermons rather than written letters. Take for instance the book of Romans. If this book were a sermon, how

---

[5] Gordon D. Fee, *Dictionary of Pentecostal and Charismatic Origins*, "Pauline Literature," Grand Rapids: Zondervan Publishing House), 666.

long would it take to preach it? According to my research, it would take about 52 minutes.[6] This is about the length of an average class period in a typical Bible school. According to my reading of this "sermon," Paul mentions, or makes direct reference to, the work of the Holy Spirit at least twenty-eight times, as follows:

1. 1:1 "the Spirit of holiness"
2. 1:11 "some spiritual gift"
3. 2:29 "circumcision ... by the Spirit"
4. 5:5 "the love of God has been poured out ... by the Holy Spirit"
5. 8:2 "the law of the Spirit of life"
6. 8:4 "live ... according to the Spirit"
7. 8:5 "who live in accordance with the Spirit"
8. 8:5 "what the Spirit desires"
9. 8:6 "the mind controlled by the Spirit"
10. 8:9 "controlled ... by the Spirit"
11. 8:9 "the Spirit of God lives in you"
12. 8:9 "the Spirit of Christ"
13. 8:10 "the Spirit is life because of righteousness" (KJV)
14. 8:11 "the Spirit of him who raised Jesus from the dead"
15. 8:11 "through his Spirit who lives in you"
16. 8:13 "by the Spirit put to death the misdeeds of the body"
17. 8:14 "led by the Spirit of God"
18. 8:15 "the Spirit of sonship"
19. 8:16 "the Spirit Himself testifies with our spirit"
20. 8:23 "the first fruits of the Spirit"
21. 8:26 "the Spirit helps us in our weakness"
22. 8:26 "the Spirit himself intercedes for us"

---

[6] The length of the sermon would, of course, vary according to the presenter's rate of speech. I believe, however, that this is a good "average" time.

23. 8:27   "the mind of the Spirit"
24. 8:27   "the Spirit intercedes for the saints"
25. 9:1   "my conscience confirms it in the Holy Spirit"
26. 14:17 "righteousness, peace and joy in the Holy Spirit"
27. 15:13 "hope by the power of the Holy Spirit"
28. 15:19 "signs and miracles, through the power of the Spirit"
29. 15:30 "the love of the Spirit"

Now, consider with me for a moment. If this were a 52 minute sermon, this would mean that in this sermon Paul mentions the Holy Spirit, on the average, every 1.85 minutes. This finding becomes even more significant when you consider another fact. Paul did not write this letter to teach about the work of the Holy Spirit in the life of the believer. He wrote to teach about salvation through faith in Jesus Christ. The theme of this letter is God's sovereign plan of salvation. So, here in Paul's "salvation sermon" he mentions the Holy Spirit every 1.85 minutes. Incredible!

We can do the same thing with other of Paul's epistles. Take, for instance, his letter to the Galatians, whose theme is salvation by faith apart from the works of the law. According to my reckoning, if this letter were preached as a sermon, it would take about 16 minutes. Now think; if you were to hear a 16 minute sermon today on the topic justification by faith, how many times do you suppose the person of the Holy Spirit would be mentioned? Very few, indeed. But not so with Paul! In this short sermon Paul mentions the Holy Spirit no less than sixteen times as follows:

1. 3:2   "receive the Spirit"
2. 3:3   "beginning with the Spirit"
3. 3:5   "Does God give you his Spirit"
4. 3:14 "the promise of the Spirit"
5. 4:6   "the Spirit of His Son"

6.	4:29	"born by the power of the Spirit"
7.	5:5	"we eagerly await through the Spirit"
8.	5:16	"live by the Spirit"
9.	5:17	"contrary to the Spirit"
10.	5:18	"if you are led by the Spirit"
11.	5:22	"the fruit of the Spirit"
12.	5:25	"we live in the Spirit"
13.	5:25	"keep in step with the Spirit"
14.	6:1	"you who are spiritual"
15.	6:8	"the one who sows to please the Spirit"
16.	6:8	"from the Spirit reap eternal life"

This means that, on the average, Paul mentions the Holy Spirit once every 60 seconds—and this in a sermon on justification by faith!

We could do the same thing with other letters of Paul. However, rather than become tedious, we will simply report our personal findings on three other selected epistles of Paul in the chart below. For comparison value we have also included the two epistles mentioned above.

In the last three epistles listed in the chart below you will notice that Paul is dealing with three widely differing themes: church problems (1 Corinthians), the believer's position in Christ (Ephesians), and preparedness for Christ's second coming (1 Thessalonians). However, you will also notice that, even though he is dealing with a variety of subjects, Paul repeatedly makes mention of the Spirit's person and work.

Paul deals extensively with the work of the Spirit in two extended passages in Romans 8 and 1 Corinthians 12-14. In the Romans passage eighteen consecutive verses deal with the work of the Holy Spirit in the believer's sanctification (vv. 1-17). In this passage Paul makes at least nineteen direct references to the work of the Holy Spirit. In 1 Corinthians 12-14, Paul discusses the proper exercise of gifts of the Holy Spirit in the local church. Here we have 84 consecutive verses dealing with the work of the Spirit of God, with a great many direct references to the Holy Spirit and His working in and through the Spirit-filled believer.

Again, the point I am making with this detailed analysis of these selected epistles of Paul is this: Paul taught much about the Holy Spirit. Further, it seems that no matter what subject Paul was teaching on He saw the Holy Spirit as being a vital element.

SUMMARY

We have thus far demonstrated several things: We have shown that the teaching ministry of Jesus was filled with teaching about the Spirit of God. He taught often and abundantly on the subject. His life and ministry were a continual model of how to live and minister in the power of the Spirit. Much of what we know today about the Spirit's person and work, we learn directly from the teaching and example of Jesus. He often began His teaching about the Spirit with a demonstration of the Spirit's power in His own ministry. He would then take time to explain to his listeners what had happened.

Following the example of Jesus, the apostles placed great emphasis on teaching about the Holy Spirit. We see this convincingly demonstrated in the book of Acts. A primary concern of the primitive church leaders was that the new disciples who were being constantly added to the church in its international missionary efforts understood and experienced the work of the Holy Spirit in their own lives. This is shown by the fact that teaching about the Holy was at the top of their "to do" list when they arrived in any new locality.

Name of the Epistle	Theme of the Epistle	Minutes Required to "Preach"	References to the Holy Spirit	Location of References	Frequency of the Spirit's Mention
Rom.	God's sovereign plan of salvation	52 min.	28 times	Listed above	Once every 1.85 minutes
Gal.	Justification by faith apart from the works of the Law	16 min.	16 times	Listed above	Once every minute
1 Cor.	Correction for church problems and carnal living	54 min.	41 times	1:7; 2:4-5, 10-15; 3:1, 16; 5:4; 6:11, 14, 19; 7:40; 9:11; 10:3-4; 12:1, 3-4; 7, 11, 13, 28, 31; 14:1-2, 12-15, 26, 37, 39; 15:44-46	Once every 1.32 minutes
Eph.	Who we are and what we have in Christ	24 min.	16 times	1:13, 17; 2:18, 22; 3:5, 16, 20; 4:3-4, 23, 30; 5:9, 18-19; 6:17-18	Once every 1.5 minutes
1 Thes.	Holy living in light of Christ's coming	12 min.	5 times	1:5-6; 4:8; 5:19-20	Once every 2.4 minutes

Then, as we analyze the epistles of Paul, we are struck with the sheer volume of teaching about the Holy Spirit we find there. No matter what the subject, he seemed to always find a direct tie with the work of the Spirit of God. His letters are models of how teaching about the Holy Spirit should pervade our teaching in the church today.

In the next chapter we will continue our look at the Holy Spirit in the content of Pentecostal teaching. We will make practical application of the things we have learned thus far to contemporary Pentecostal teaching.

— CHAPTER 2 —

THE HOLY SPIRIT IN THE CONTENT OF CONTEMPORARY PENTECOSTAL TEACHING

In the last chapter we looked at the Holy Spirit in the content of the teaching ministry of Jesus, in the preaching and teaching of the ministries of the apostles in the book of Acts, and in the epistles of Paul. In each case we discovered that their teaching was packed with content about the Spirit of God. In this chapter we will make practical application of the things we are learning. We will look at the place of the Holy Spirit in the content of contemporary Pentecostal teaching. In order that we do not miss the point, I again state our thesis for the chapter: If Jesus and the apostles saw the vital importance of teaching much and often about the person and work of the Holy Spirit, then we, as their twenty-first century successors, should do the same.

Contemporary Pentecostal Teaching

An important question naturally arises at this point: If our teaching is to be saturated with teaching about the Holy Spirit, what exactly should we teach? As teachers in Pentecostal Bible schools we should commit ourselves to teach systematically, convincingly, and abundantly about the Holy Spirit. Without such a commitment we are not likely to produce the Spirit-anointed preachers we must have if we are to impact our societies and the world as did the early church. This teaching about the Holy Spirit can be grouped into three categories: (1) we should teach about the vital importance of the Holy Spirit; (2) we should teach about the wonderful person of the Holy Spirit; and (3) we should teach about the powerful works of the Holy Spirit.

We Should Teach about the Holy Spirit

First, we should teach about the vital importance of the Holy Spirit. Our teaching about the Holy Spirit should include, among other things, instruction on the indispensable value of the Holy Spirit to the lives and ministries of our students. These students must sense the deep conviction of his teacher: "I cannot live or minister without the Spirit's presence in my life." Further, the students must understand the critical importance of the Spirit of God to their lives. They must be inspired to live their lives in His presence, and to know and experience His power.

We, then, as Pentecostal teachers, must see it as our responsibilities to demonstrate, by word and example, how important the Holy Spirit is to the life of the Pentecostal minister. Just as Paul taught the believers in Corinth, we must teach our students to "covet" and "eagerly desire" the working of the Spirit in their lives and ministries (1 Cor. 12:31; 14:1, 39).

Second, we should teach about the wonderful Person of the Holy Spirit. Our students must know who He is. They must understand His divine nature and know His essential attributes. They must be able to appreciate that He is a wonderful divine Person who desires loving fellowship with each of them. They must understand His relationship to the Father and the Son, to mankind, and to the church. They must know and understand the profound meaning of His names and titles. Our students must understand these things in order that they may be motivated to know and serve Him better, and live in a vital living relationship with Him.

Finally, we should teach about the powerful works of the Holy Spirit. We should teach our students about His works in creation, in the inspiration of Scripture, and in the anointing of the Old Testament prophets, priests, and kings. We should teach them about His work in the life of the Lord Jesus Christ and in the New Testament believers. We should teach them about His present work in the lives of believers: infilling, anointing, inspiring, cleansing, revealing, enlightening, interceding, calling, comforting, healing, helping, teaching, counseling, empowering, illuminating, and gifting.

We must teach them these things in order that our students may be able hear His voice, know His anointing, and release His gifts in their ministries. We must teach them how to discern the Spirit's presence, how to hear the Spirit's voice, how to yield to the Spirit's anointing, and how to release the Spirit's gifts. If we teach them any less, we cannot honestly say that we are adequately equipping them for a truly Pentecostal ministry.

A Response Demanded

This brings us to another important question, "What should our response be to the things we have thus far learned?" Certainly, such new insight demands a personal response. But what must that response be? Like Jesus and the apostles, we must give the Holy Spirit His proper place of ascendancy in our lives and in our teaching. This applies both to us who are administrators and to us who are teachers in Pentecostal Bibles schools. First I would like to speak to Bible school administrators, and then I would like to speak to Bible school teachers.

As Administrators in Pentecostal Bible Schools

Those of us who serve as administrators of Pentecostal Bible schools must reexamine our schools curricula candidly asking ourselves probing questions:

- Does our curricula really reflect a proper emphasis on the person and work of the Holy Spirit?
- Does it reflect a truly Pentecostal emphasis?

By a truly Pentecostal emphasis I am not talking about an occasional course on "Pneumatology" or "Spiritual Gifts." What I am asking is this: Is our curricula fashioned to train effective Pentecostal ministers? Has it been thoughtfully designed to produce men and women with a thorough understanding of the proper role of the Holy Spirit in their own lives and ministries—that is, men and women who can move and minister in the power and anointing of the Spirit? In my personal examination of the curricula of several Pentecostal Bible schools, it appears that this is not the case. In far too many cases we see little more that a typical non-Pentecostal evangelical curriculum with a smattering of "Pentecostal" offerings.

A brief historical review of Bible school training in the Pentecostal movement will help us to understand better. Historically there have been at least three major Bible school models used in the Pentecostal/charismatic communities. I call these three models the "Faith Bible School" model, the "Bible Institute" model, and a more recent addition, the "Charismatic" model.

The Faith Bible School Model

The first model, the Faith Bible School model, was the primary training model of the Pentecostal movement in its infancy. Today this model has been largely abandoned by the major Pentecostal denominations. An example of such a school was the Bethel Bible School of Topeka, Kansas, USA, founded by Charles F. Parham. It was there where many historians believe the modern Pentecostal movement had its theological beginnings. Another such school was founded by early Pentecostal leader D. W. Myland, and another by D. C. O. Opperman, one of the founding fathers of the Assemblies of God. In most of these schools the Bible was the only textbook. The teaching plan most frequently used in these schools was topical studies. A topic was chosen and then a search was made by the student body of the entire Bible to shed light on the subject. Their findings were then discussed in class. These schools were short-termed, often lasting only a few weeks.

These faith schools had both their weaknesses and their strengths. Their weaknesses included such things as the scarcity or total lack of textbooks, the absence of a well-thought-out curricula, and their transient nature due to the lack of permanent facilities. However, they also had their notable strengths. Among these was an atmosphere characterized by living faith, active service, and zealous prayer. The presence of the Spirit could be felt and seen in the frequent manifestations of spiritual gifts. Lewis F. Wilson, professor of history at Southern California College, in Costa Mesa, California, (now Vanguard University) wrote concerning these early faith Bible schools:

> Although the limitations of such schools were obvious, they did provide basic training in Pentecostal beliefs and experience. The stated purpose of Opperman's schools was to learn "How to pray, how to study the word, and how to know God and walk with Him" (*Word and Witness*, December 20,

1913). Classes were sometimes interrupted by spontaneous prayer, praise, and the exercise of spiritual gifts. Some of the distinctive aspects of Pentecostal worship apparently developed in these classes. Certainly some of the future Pentecostal pastors and leaders received their training at such schools.[7]

In these schools there was also a distinct emphasis on practical application. Wilson points out that these schools "emphasized practical training and personal piety more than academic excellence."[8] Afternoons and weekends were often spent in street evangelism and witnessing. The students' schedules were filled with times of extended prayer and seeking God.

Other more permanent schools followed much the same "strictly Bible" curricula. With a two-year program, the Rochester Bible Training School, Rochester, New York, was one such school. Subjects taught included book surveys, evangelism, homiletics, exegesis, and missionary work. During its eighteen years in existence the school in Rochester graduated more than 400 students, including 50 foreign missionaries.[9]

The Bible Institute Model

A second model of ministerial training used by Pentecostals is the Bible Institute model. With the passing of time the Pentecostal Bible schools expanded and developed their programs. Following World War II, there came a movement toward

---

[7] Lewis F. Wilson, *Dictionary of Pentecostal and Charismatic Origins*, "Bible Institutes, Colleges, Universities" (Grand Rapids: Zondervan, 1988), 59.

[8] Ibid. 60.

[9] Ibid. 59.

accreditation on the part of major Pentecostal Bible schools across the USA. Accreditation agencies demanded that these schools expand their curricula. As curricula and programs were expanded, this second training model developed within the Pentecostal movement. This model remains a dominant model used by the major Pentecostal denominations around the world. This model follows the pattern set by such schools as Moody Bible Institute of Chicago, Illinois, [10] It has as its primary goal a well-rounded and broad-based curriculum covering a wide range of Biblical and ministerial topics. Many Pentecostal schools have adopted this model almost in toto—with the addition of a few selected courses on Pentecostal themes.

Like the Faith Bible School model this model has its strengths and weaknesses. A great strength of this model is its comprehensive coverage of the Bible and ministerial topics. The student completing such a curriculum can boast of having a thoroughgoing biblical and ministerial education. It's weakness, at least from the Pentecostal perspective, is that it places only a superficial emphasis on the person and work of the Spirit, and on practical training in Pentecostal ministry. This is to be expected, since it was never intended to service a Pentecostal constituency.

Through the years Pentecostal educators have tried, with limited success, to remedy this deficiency by adding selected "Pentecostal" courses to the curriculum. In my opinion, however, this system has proven to be inadequate in training Pentecostal ministers. Far too often the graduates of these institutions, while Pentecostal by profession, are often lacking the doctrinal foundation and spiritual dynamic needed for a truly Pentecostal/charismatic ministry. Some contend that because of the

---

[10] William W. Menzies, *Anointed to Serve* (Springfield, MO: Gospel Publishing House, 1971), 354.

quest for accreditation and the resulting demands of accreditation agencies on the curricula of our schools, our schools have become too "secularized" and this had contributed to, what one writer has called the "domestication of Pentecostalism."

The Neo-Pentecostal or Charismatic Model

A third model of ministerial training used by the Pentecostal/charismatic community is what I call the Neo-Pentecostal or Charismatic model. The emergence of these schools was, in part, a reaction among charismatics and some Pentecostals to what they believed was the secularization of Pentecostal Bible schools. These people believed that the early unaccredited Bible institutes had better served the needs of the movement. One example of such a school is Christ for the Nations Institute in Dallas, Texas, founded by in 1970 by Gordon Lindsay, longtime leader in the American healing movement. This two-year Bible-based program has a strong emphasis on evangelism and missions. In just over one decade the school grew from just 45 to more than 1,500 students.

Other schools were established to propagate the unique emphases of their founders. One such school is Rhema Bible Training Center in Tulsa, Oklahoma, founded by Kenneth Hagin.

These schools also have their strengths and weaknesses. One strength is the fact that they seem to be tapping into a responsive chord in the Pentecostal/charismatic community—the desire for a greater understanding of the things of God. Another strength is the single-minded purpose of many of these schools. Because they are often controlled by one man, one church, or a small group of like-minded people, they are able to maintain a clear focus on their reason for being. These schools do, however, also have their glaring weaknesses. They are often susceptible to the latest doctrinal fad sweeping the charismatic community. Another weakness is the fact that these schools often find their center in a dominating personality rather than the larger Pentecostal/charismatic community.

Needed, A Contemporary Pentecostal Model

What we must develop in Africa (and around the world), I am convinced, is a well-considered contemporary Pentecostal model for the training Spirit-filled pastors and church leaders. We must reexamine what we are doing, asking penetrating questions about our purposes and methods. We must also ask probing questions concerning our training institutions. What kind of product are they producing? Are the graduates of these institutions truly anointed men and women of God, fully equipped to preach and teach our distinctive Pentecostal message? Have they been adequately prepared to effectively preach the gospel to the ends of the earth in the power of the Holy Spirit?

As we develop this contemporary Pentecostal model of ministerial training, we must hold to the best and most productive things we are doing. However, we must go beyond that. We must think and act boldly and creatively. We could begin by choosing the best features of the above and other models, and rejecting anything that does not help us reach our goal of thoroughly-trained, spiritually-equipped Pentecostal ministers. Next, we must reexamine our present curricula to see if they are effective in the training of a truly Pentecostal ministry, or are they just hastily adjusted imitations of other, often non-Pentecostal, programs.

In my observation, in most "Pentecostal" curricula there are far too few courses dealing with subjects essential to Pentecostal ministry. Two or three courses on Pentecostal themes in a three or four-year program is woefully inadequate for producing the product that we desire—truly Pentecostal ministers who are focused on reaching the nations with the gospel and able to minister in the power and anointing of the Spirit. An occasional course on "Pneumatology" or "Pentecostal Doctrine" will never suffice. We must rather "Pentecostalize" and "missionize" every course taught in our ministerial training institutions. By this I mean that we must reexamine every course, no matter what the subject, to ensure that each contains the necessary pneumatological and missiological emphasis. Our experience with the Holy Spirit should affect everything we do and teach.

I remember how the late Dr. John York, founder of Africa's Hope, an Assemblies of God missionary agency aimed at facilitating ministerial training in the Assemblies of God in Africa, was very serious about this issue. Early in the process of developing the Discovery Series textbooks for our African Bible schools, he solicited my help. I was asked to review each textbook, evaluating its Pentecostal and missional emphasis and make suggestions for change, which were then presented to the curriculum committee for final approval.

One my last and fondest memories of John is the day that he and I spent in his office reviewing the *Old Testament Survey* textbook to ensure that it had the proper Pentecostal and missional emphasis. We were both feeling ill that day. He was suffering from the effects of the leukemia, which ultimately took His life, and I with a chronic headache. He sat slumped over his desk reading aloud from the *Old Testament Survey* textbook; I lay on the couch in his office with my baseball cap pulled down over my eyes to shield them from the light. In spite of our discomfort John kept insisting that we complete the review of the book. We occasionally paused to laugh at ourselves and discuss how comical we would have appeared to someone who walked into the office. Nevertheless, at John's insistence, we persevered until our work was completed. John was uncompromising in his belief that every textbook in our African curriculum must have a clear Pentecostal and missiological emphasis.

In addition to reviewing our present current curricula for Pentecostal and missional emphasis, we further need a bold infusion of courses specifically aimed at equipping students to live and minister in the power and anointing of the Holy Spirit. A list of such needed courses must contain the following:

1. The Kingdom of God. A correct understanding of the nature and purpose of the kingdom of God is an essential foundation for any Pentecostal ministry. According to Pentecostal educator Peter Kuzmic,

> The idea of the kingdom of God occupies a place of supreme importance in the teaching and mission of Jesus. This 'master-thought' of Jesus ... is the central theme of his proclamation, and the key to understanding his ministry... [it is] the key message he instructed his disciples to proclaim when he sent them on missions (Matt.10:7; Luke 9:2; 10:9,11).[11]

A proper understanding of the power and gifts of the Holy Spirit is dependent on a proper understanding of the coming of the kingdom of God. A study of the kingdom of God seems to be an essential requisite of any truly Pentecostal curriculum.

2. Spiritual Dynamics. An experience-based course dealing with such subjects as how to pray, how to hear and know the voice of God, how to walk and live in the Holy Spirit, how to live in holiness, etc., also seems to me to be an essential part of the training of a Pentecostal clergy.

---

[11] Peter Kuzmic, *Dictionary of Pentecostal and Charismatic Movements,* "Kingdom of God" (Grand Rapids: Zondervan, 1988), 522-523.

3. Power Ministry. A practical course on how to minister in the power and anointing of the Holy Spirit is needed. Our students must know how to confront and cast out demons, how to heal the sick, and how to lead people into the baptism in the Holy Spirit.

4. The Baptism in the Holy Spirit. An entire course dealing comprehensively with the baptism in the Holy Spirit should be considered basic training for the Pentecostal minister. A proper understanding of the gift's missional nature and purpose will give essential direction to the preacher and to the movement during this present era of theological and experiential drift. Lukan Pneumatology and its implications for spiritual life and ministry should be addressed. This course must also contain a strong element on the empowering work of the Spirit in accomplishing the mission of God.

5. Pentecostal Preaching. Our present courses in homiletics need to be reviewed and revised. This course should deal extensively with the role of the Holy Spirit in preaching. The prophetic element in preaching should be explored and demonstrated as well as the "prophethood" of all believers.

6. Spiritual Gifts. Our students must understand that being Pentecostal means more than just clapping their hands and speaking in tongues. They must know how to respond to God in releasing spiritual gifts in their own ministries. This course should be very practical. It should not only dispense information about the gifts of the Spirit, but there should be a demonstration of the gifts. The students should not just be told about the spiritual gifts, but they should be shown how the gifts operate and given the opportunity to open themselves to God to allow the gifts to be manifested in their own lives and ministries.

7. An Interpretative History of the Pentecostal Movement. Our Pentecostal pastors need an understanding of their Pentecostal roots and heritage. This course should include a survey of the charismata throughout the history of the Church as well as the missional history of the church. It should examine the origin and development of the Pentecostal movement. A history of the Pentecostal movement in the continent, region, and country of the students should be written and taught. Pentecostal leaders should be able to interpret their history, not just to recite it.

8. *Faith Dynamics.* Our students must be taught how to live and move in dynamic faith. They must understand the essence of faith and also the dynamics of the faith-life. We must not shy away from this essential subject just because others have taken extreme and unscriptural stances on the same.

9. *Divine Healing.* Divine healing is one of the four cardinal doctrines of the modern Pentecostal movement. Our students must understand the biblical doctrine of divine healing; however, doctrinal understanding is not enough. This course should also examine the healing ministry of Jesus and the New Testament church in order to develop an effective model for today. This, as well as all of the courses listed here, must be combined with well-designed practicums in order that the students may be "doers of the Word and not hearers only."

10. *Pentecostal Apologetics.* What I am calling for here is a course in hermeneutics from a clearly Pentecostal perspective. By that I mean a hermeneutic that clearly and biblically answers the challenges of recent evangelical scholars from both inside and outside the movement who challenge the validity of using the writings of Luke—specifically the Acts of the Apostles—as a ground for formulating normative doctrine. Such a Pentecostal hermeneutic would also emphasize the active role of the Holy Spirit in the interpretive process.

Other Important Issues

Spiritual Formation. In addition to examining the place of the

Holy Spirit in the curricula of our schools, we, as Pentecostal Bible school administrators, must address another important issue. If we are to train truly Pentecostal ministers, we must take seriously the importance of the spiritual formation that can and must occur in our school's chapel services. This daily service in our Bible schools must be more than just a devotional time, or even worse, a time for school announcements. It must become a dynamic spiritual laboratory where students encounter the living God and learn how to respond to and move in the power of the Holy Spirit. This cannot be done in a fifteen to thirty minute chapel time. An hour or more must be allotted for this daily encounter with the Spirit. Again, we must return to our Pentecostal roots, where the spiritual atmosphere of the school was of primary importance. William Menzies describes these early Pentecostal schools:

> The ethos of the school was designed to be an intense spiritual atmosphere, an atmosphere created by scheduling numerous prayer meetings and worship services throughout the week. The center of gravity was spiritual development rather than academic excellence.[12]

Teacher Staffing. Finally, if we are to have truly Pentecostal schools, we as administrators, must look at the staffing of these schools. We must ask the critical question, "Are our present teachers able to deal adequately with this new contemporary Pentecostal paradigm?" If the answer is no, then intensive retraining is needed. When hiring new teaching staff, we must look beyond mere academic qualifications to spiritual giftedness and professional competence. Whether we realize it or not, most of our training is done by example rather than by formal instruction. Only spiritually competent teachers can produce the spiritually

---

[12] Menzies, 354-355.

competent graduates that the task of spiritual ministry demands.

As Teachers in Pentecostal Bible Schools

This brings us to our teachers in our Pentecostal Bible schools. As teachers of Pentecostal pastors, we, too, must concern ourselves with the presence of the Holy Spirit in the content of our teaching. We must be prepared to adjust the content of our lessons to conform to the biblical model presented in this chapter. Like our biblical and historical antecedents, our teaching should be filled with teaching about the person and work of the Holy Spirit. This is especially true for us whose God-given task is the training of Pentecostal ministers.

Teaching about the Holy Spirit must be viewed by every Pentecostal teacher as a matter of first importance. In order to impact our student pastors with the importance of the subject, our lessons, no matter what biblical subject, should be saturated with teaching about the blessed Holy Spirit. Each time we teach, or re-teach, a given subject, we must review our teaching notes, asking ourselves the question, "Where is the Holy Spirit and His mission in my teaching? Is what I am teaching, and how I am teaching it, adequate for preparing Pentecostal ministers?" If the answer is no, we must be willing to "begin again at the beginning" and rewrite our lessons, giving the Holy Spirit and the mission of God their proper place in their midst.

In the next chapter we will take another step in our discussion of the work of the Spirit in our teaching ministries. We will discuss the importance of the Holy Spirit's presence in the context of our Pentecostal teaching.

— CHAPTER 3 —

The Holy Spirit in the Context

of Pentecostal Teaching

Someone has correctly observed that teaching is more than talking, and learning is more than listening. Beyond talking, teaching involves being, modeling, demonstrating, and imparting. And beyond listening, learning involves observing, doing, and becoming. In fact, we often teach more when we are not teaching (that is, in the formal act of teaching) than when we are teaching. In other words, we teach more by who we are and by what we do than by what we say. We teach by simply being a man or woman of God, and, then, being with our students. As they observe our life and works, they become like us. Jesus, the Master Teacher, taught us, "Everyone who is fully trained will be like his teacher" (Luke 6:40). When Jesus called the twelve to Himself and appointed them as apostles, He did it so that "they might be with Him" (Mark 3:14). Robert E. Coleman has observed,

Having called His men, Jesus made it a practice to be with them. This was the essence of His training program—just letting His disciple follow Him... Jesus had no formal school, no Seminaries, no outlined course of study... None of these highly organized procedures considered so necessary today entered in at all into His ministry. Amazing as it may seem, all Jesus did to teach these men His way was to draw them close to Himself. He was His own school and curriculum.[13]

As teachers, we must know that we teach primarily by our lives. One veteran teacher said it well: "We cannot not teach." As teachers, everything we are and do teaches a lesson to our students. Even when we don't do anything, our inactivity teaches our students something about our goals and values.

In Chapters 1 and 2 we talked about the place of the Holy Spirit in the content of Pentecostal teaching. In this chapter we will take the next step. We will talk about the role of the Holy Spirit in the *context* of Pentecostal teaching. Pentecostal Bible school teachers who truly desires to teach *in the Spirit* should be concerned with more than just the content of their lessons, they must also concern themselves with their context.

CONTEXT, ITS DEFINITION AND IMPORTANCE

What do we mean by the context of Pentecostal teaching? By context we are talking about the environment surrounding a particular teaching session. This would include the cultural context, the classroom setup, the spiritual level of the institution, the attitudes of the teacher and students, and many other factors.

---

[13]Robert E. Coleman, *The Master Plan of Evangelism* (Old Tappan, New Jersey: Fleming H. Revell Co., 1987), 38.

Jesus understood the importance of context to ministry. In His healing ministry Jesus often concerned Himself with the "healing environment" surrounding a particular ministry action. One example of this is found in His healing of Jairus' daughter (Mark 5). As the story begins a synagogue ruler by the name of Jairus accosts Jesus and pleads with Him to come to his house and heal his little daughter, who is at the point of death. Jesus immediately responds and goes with the distraught father. En route, He is delayed by a woman, who is also in desperate need. While Jairus nervously waits, Jesus takes time to minister to her need. Then, before he finishes ministering to this woman, a delegation of men arrive from the house of Jairus. Their message is devastating: "Your daughter is dead. Why bother the Teacher anymore?" (v. 35). Jesus immediately begins to take charge of the spiritual environment. He turns and speaks words of faith to the girl's father, "Don't be afraid," He says, "just believe" (v. 36). Upon arriving at the home of Jairus, Jesus encounters a group of mourners weeping and wailing. Again, He takes control of the spiritual environment: He puts them all out of the house. He then raises the girl from the dead and presents her alive to her parents. Jesus understood the critical importance of the spiritual context in a ministry encounter.

A thoughtful reexamination of the four gospels reveals that Jesus frequently did the same in His teaching ministry. For example:

> That same day Jesus went out of the house and sat by the lake. Such large crowds gathered around him that he got into a boat and sat in it, while all the people stood on the shore. (Matt. 13:1-2)

Here Jesus arranged the physical environment of a teaching situation. Before teaching the multitudes He set the stage for the teaching event. Later in the chapter He does it again:

> Then he left the crowd and went into the house. His disciples came to him and said, "Explain to us the parable on the weeds in the field." He answered ... (vv. 36-37)

Here, before teaching His disciples, Jesus again tends to the teaching environment. He sends the crowds away, and takes his students into a house where He can teach them privately.

On yet another occasion, in preparation for teaching a lesson on prayer, Jesus created the necessary spiritual environment:

> One day Jesus was praying in a certain place. When he finished, one of his disciples said to him, "Lord, teach us to pray as John taught his disciples." He said to them... (Luke 11:1-2)

Through the example of His own prayer life, Jesus set the stage for teaching His disciples about prayer. He whetted their spiritual appetites, creating in them the desire for the kind of intimate relationship with God that they had seen in Him. He waited for them to ask for help, then He began teaching them how to pray.

On yet another occasion Jesus taught the Seventy-two and sent them out on a ministry assignment—what could be called a first-century teaching practicum (Luke 10:1-16). The Seventy-two returned with a glowing report: "Lord, even the demons submit to us in Your name" (v. 17). Seeing that the moment was right, Jesus began to teach them. He taught them concerning the eventual overthrow and defeat of Satan's kingdom, their imputed power and authority over demons, and the importance of humility in a power ministry (vv.18-20). At this moment the Holy Spirit came upon Jesus, and in the presence of these students, He began to rejoice in the Spirit (v. 21). Think how this simple act must have affected His disciples. He then turned to them and said,

Blessed are the eyes that see what you see. For I tell you that many prophets and kings wanted to see what you see but did not see it, and hear what you hear but did not hear it. (vv. 23-24)

We can only imagine the profound effect of this teaching encounter on the disciples. Jesus had picked the perfect moment to teach His disciples—when the context was just right for what He wanted to say.

It would be difficult to overstate the importance of context in the training of Pentecostal ministers. We must constantly remind ourselves that we are training, not just religious lecturers, but men and women who must know how to minister the Word of God in the Spirit's power. Further, we must realize that the student often learns more from the context of the lesson than from its content.

The context of Jesus' training of the Twelve was dominated by His physical presence. This was the controlling factor in His teaching environment. Their being with Him changed them! When the disciples eventually went out on their own, the people "realized what being with Jesus had done for them!" (Acts 4:13, TLB).

As in His teaching, the dominating factor in our teaching must also be the manifest presence of Christ through the Holy Spirit. Paul referred to the Holy Spirit as "the Spirit of Christ" (Rom. 8:9). He is the one who reveals Christ to the world. Before His death Jesus told His disciples, "I will not leave you as orphans; I will come to you..." (John 14:18). This was a promise of the coming of the Holy Spirit—the Helper, who would take Jesus' place (14:26; 15:26; 16:7). Where the presence of the Holy Spirit is, there also is the presence of Jesus. It is noteworthy that in John 14:26 Jesus said that the Holy Spirit would come as the Teacher. Clearly, then, the presence of the Holy Spirit must be a dominant feature of the context of Pentecostal training.

BIBLICAL EXAMPLES: THE HOLY SPIRIT IN THE CONTEXT OF NEW TESTAMENT TEACHING

If we are to take the teaching ministry of Jesus and the apostles as our model for Pentecostal teaching today, we too, must concern ourselves with the presence of the Holy Spirit in the teaching environment. So that we may better understand that environment, let's now look at some examples of the Holy Spirit in the context of Jesus' teaching, and then in the teaching ministry of the New Testament church.

The Holy Spirit in the Context of Jesus' Teaching

Concerning His own teaching ministry Jesus said, "The Spirit gives life; the flesh counts for nothing; the words I have spoken to you are spirit and they are life" (John 6:63). Jesus seems to be saying that in His teaching His very words bore the presence of the Spirit. Or, as Robert E. Tourville says, "It is as though the breath of God breathes on man through Jesus' words, thus bringing life to the dead."[14]

The environment in which Jesus taught was impregnated with the presence and power of the Spirit. Three examples taken from the gospel of Luke make this point. In them we observe a powerful presence of the Holy Spirit in the context of Jesus' teaching ministry. In each we will note how the Spirit's presence filled the environment as Jesus taught. The first example is found in Luke 4: 14-15:

---

[14] Robert E. Tourville, *The Complete Biblical Library, John* (Springfield, MO: World Library Press, 1991), 183.

> Jesus returned to Galilee in the power of the Spirit, and news about Him spread through the whole countryside. He taught in their synagogues, and everyone praised Him.

Note how Jesus taught "in the power of the Spirit" in their synagogues. The teaching environment was pregnant with the Spirit's presence.

Another incident shows even more clearly how Jesus taught in the context of the Spirit's manifest presence:

> One day as he was teaching, Pharisees and teachers of the law, who had come from every village of Galilee and from Judea and Jerusalem, were sitting there. And the power of the Lord was present for him to heal the sick. (Luke 5:17)

Note the two phrases: "... as he was teaching ... the power of the Lord was present."

From these two examples we learn that the context of Jesus' teaching was not the sterile, lifeless environment that characterizes far too many present-day Bible school classes. As Jesus taught, there was a clearly discernible presence of the Spirit of God. Such a Presence should also mark our Pentecostal classrooms today.

A final example of the Holy Spirit in the context of Jesus' teaching is found in an impromptu teaching session in which Jesus taught on, among other things, spiritual warfare and the sin of blaspheming the Holy Spirit (Luke 11:17-26).[15] We will not, however, focus on the content of His teaching, but the context. The context for this teaching session was a power encounter between Jesus and a virulent demon causing its host to be both deaf and

---

[15] You will recall that we have already discussed this incident in Jesus' life in Chapter 1 using the parallel passage, Matt. 12:22-28.

mute. Jesus drove the demon out of a man, thus freeing him from his deaf-mutism. This healing caused a controversy between those who thought He could be the long-awaited Jewish Messiah and those who thought He was an agent of Beelzebub.

Through the Spirit Jesus was made aware of their thoughts. It was in this context, the context of the manifestation of two gifts of the Spirit—the first a power gift, the second a revelation gift—that Jesus began to teach the people about the person and work of the Holy Spirit. Again, we note a pervasive presence of the Holy Spirit as the context of Jesus' teaching ministry.[16]

In the above examples we discover that when Jesus taught the atmosphere was often infused with the manifest presence of the Holy Spirit. This presence was often demonstrated through the release of spiritual gifts in His ministry. It should be the goal of every Pentecostal teacher today that such a manifest presence of the Holy Spirit marks his or her teaching ministry.

Understand, I am not saying that there should be a visible display of spiritual power in every class session. I am saying, however, that our students should be able to sense the presence of the Holy Spirit as we teach them. And, as we teach on such things as the dynamics of the Holy Spirit in the life of the minister and the church, our verbal teaching should be accompanied by a demonstration of the Spirit's presence and power. Any less will fail to produce the results required in the lives of our students.

The Holy Spirit in the Context of the Apostle's Teaching

As we move from the gospels into the book of Acts we can see that the Holy Spirit was also present in the context of the teaching ministry of the New Testament church. In Acts the Holy

---

[16] Another example of the manifestation of spiritual gifts during a teaching session of Jesus is found in Mark 1:21-27.

Spirit dominates the teaching environment. On the Day of Pentecost, Peter's prophetic teaching to the multitudes was preceded by a powerful demonstration of the Spirit's presence (Acts 2:1-4). In the city of Ephesus, after teaching on the subject of the Holy Spirit, Paul laid hands on his "class members" and "the Holy Spirit came on them, and they spoke with tongues and prophesied" (19:6). He was not satisfied that his students had filled their notebooks with lecture notes, he knew that their lives must be filled with the presence and power of the Spirit of God. Paul reminded the Corinthian believers of His charismatic teaching ministry in their city:

> My message [the words I spoke] and my preaching were not with wise and persuasive words, but with a demonstration of the Spirit's power, so that your faith might not rest on men's wisdom, but on God's power. (1 Cor. 2:4-5)

Note carefully that Paul does not say that his preaching and teaching ministry were *accompanied by* a demonstration of God's power (of which there is no doubt), but that his actual words were a demonstration of God's power. We are reminded of the words of Jesus: "The words that I speak, they are Spirit." Is it any wonder that the words of Jesus and Paul so dramatically affected their hearers? And, is it any wonder that so much of our modern-day teaching falls on dull ears?

Paul viewed teaching as a charismatic event. By a "charismatic event" I mean an event that includes the manifestation of a spiritual dynamic. A thoughtful observation of Paul's list of spiritual gifts at the end of 1 Corinthians 12 yields an interesting insight: teaching is a charismatic gift of the Holy Spirit: "And in the church God has appointed first of all apostles, second prophets, third teachers, then workers of miracles, also those having gifts of healing..." (v. 28)

Note how, in this passage, the gift of teaching is listed, with no qualifications, among such gifts as apostle, prophet, miracles, and healings. The implication is that same Holy Spirit should be actively at work in the ministry of the teacher as He is in the ministry of the apostle, the prophet, the healer, or the worker of miracles.

Again, in the same context, the apostle lists the gift of teaching among other more obviously charismatic gifts:

> What shall we say brothers? When you come together, everyone has a hymn, or a word of instruction, a revelation, a tongue or an interpretation. All of these must be done for the strengthening of the church. (1 Cor. 14:26)

Paul's obvious implication is that all of these manifestations of the Spirit, including a "word of instruction," are operations of the same Holy Spirit. Further, according to this text, teaching takes place in the context of such things as tongues, interpretation, and revelation, and should be inspired and anointed by the same Holy Spirit. Such a manifest presence of the Spirit should also mark the Pentecostal classroom today.

Paul informed the Romans of his method of "leading the Gentiles to obey God" (Rom. 15:18). He did it, he said, "by what I have said and done." He, then, points out that, whether he ministered in word or in deed, he did it all "through the power of the Spirit" (v. 19). In other words, the "signs and miracles" that accompanied his apostolic ministry, as well as his teaching and preaching, were all done through the power and anointing of the Spirit of God.

Remember, when the Holy Spirit comes into our classrooms, He comes to assist us. He comes to *teach*. The night before His crucifixion Jesus told his disciples:

> But the Counselor, the Holy Spirit, whom the Father will send in my name, will teach you all things and will remind you of everything I have said to you. (John 14:26).

He spoke further on the same subject. "I have much to say to you, more than you can now bear," He said, "but when he, the Spirit of truth, comes, he will guide you into all truth. (16:12-13)
So, when the Divine Teacher comes, we should let Him teach! The anointing is given to us—and our students—that we might know more fully the things of God, things that can only be spiritually discerned (1 Cor.2:14). John taught concerning this anointing from God:

> But you have an anointing from the Holy One, and all of you know the truth... As for you, the anointing you received from him remains in you, and you do not need anyone to teach you. But his anointing teaches you about all things and as that anointing is real, not counterfeit—just as it has taught you, remain in him. (1 John 2:20, 27).

John was not advocating that, because we have the Spirit of God, we no longer need teachers, and should thus dispense with them. After all, John was teaching them at that very moment! And teaching is one of the gifts given by the Spirit of God. What John was saying is that, since we have the Spirit, we should not fall prey to false teachers ("antichrists," v. 18) as others had done. He was also saying that the anointing that we have from God teaches us about the things of God.

What conclusion can we draw from these examples concerning the context of teaching in the New Testament? We conclude that it was not a sterile, lifeless environment, but one alive with the presence of the Holy Spirit—an environment often saturated with the manifest presence of God. The lessons that they taught were relevant, and the words that they spoke were anointed by the Spirit of God. Spiritual gifts often accompanied and undergirded their teaching, demonstrating that God was truly alive and present. Because of these things their hearers were dramatically transformed into men and women able to live and move in the Spirit's presence and power.

OUR RESPONSE: WHAT THEN SHOULD THE CONTEXT OF OUR TEACHING LOOK LIKE?

As I close this chapter, I ask one final question: What should our response be to these things we have learned? Or, stated another way, if we are to be Pentecostal trainers of Pentecostal ministers, what should the context of our teaching look like? In a word, the context of our teaching should mirror the biblical pattern. We should do it like Jesus did it, and like His disciples did it after Him.

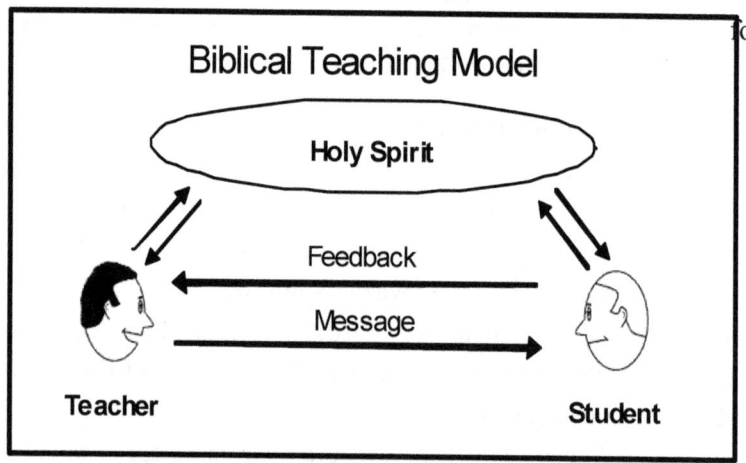

Figure 2: Biblical Teaching Model

The context of our teaching should be saturated with the presence the blessed Third Person of the Trinity.

For far too long, we who call ourselves Pentecostal teachers have been content with a non-Pentecostal model for teaching. Often our model has even been secular, totally lacking any divine presence or dynamic. In such a model, as the teacher teaches, he or she receives and responds to the feedback from the students. There is a reciprocal communication between teacher and students, as is illustrated in Figure 1.

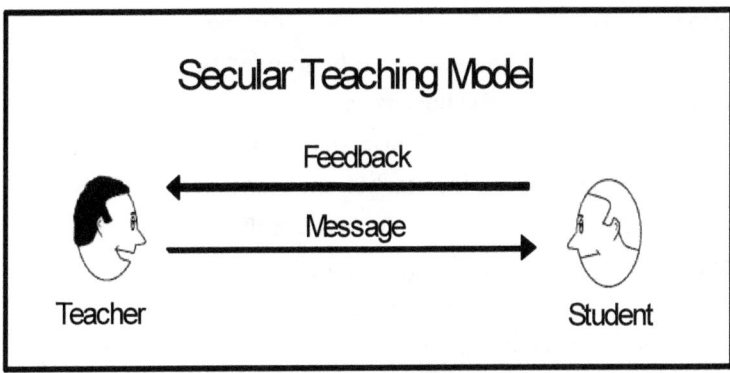

Figure 1: Secular Teaching Model

This model, however, falls short of the biblical ideal. In the biblical model there is the same give and take between the teacher and the pupil; however, there is an added dynamic, the manifest presence of the Holy Spirit, as is shown in Figure 2 (next page).

You will notice that, in this model, not only is there an interplay between the teacher and students, but there is also a give and take between the teacher and the Holy Spirit. There is further a give and take between the students and the Holy Spirit. Such a model is essential for the training of Pentecostal ministers of the gospel.

CONCLUSION

We conclude that the context of Pentecostal teaching should include at least three essential elements. First, it should include the manifest presence of God. The teacher and student alike should be able to sense the presence of the Spirit of God. Often this Presence is the most life-changing element of the lesson.

Second the context of Pentecostal teaching should include an appropriate response to that divine Presence. When the Spirit comes, we must not ignore Him! We must gladly welcome Him into our classroom and give Him the honor He is due. How many times has the Spirit come only to be grieved because we ignored Him? May this never be the case as we teach.

And finally, when the Spirit comes, there must be a continual give and take between the teacher, the students, and the Spirit of God. Both teacher and student must have their spiritual eyes open to see what the Spirit is doing, and their spiritual ears open to hear what He is saying. We must never forget that we are Pentecostal trainers of Pentecostal ministers. We must always give the Spirit of God the preeminent place in our classrooms.

In the next chapter we will discuss the role of the Holy Spirit in the presentation of Pentecostal teaching.

— CHAPTER 4 —

The Holy Spirit in the Presentation

of Pentecostal Teaching

Thus far in our study we have demonstrated that the Holy Spirit must be given his proper place in both the content and in the context of our teaching. In this chapter we will take a final step and propose that the Holy Spirit must also be present in the *presentation* of truly New Testament teaching. I will attempt to answer the question, "What role should be the Holy Spirit play in the teacher himself or herself as they present their lesson?"

Not only should the Spirit of God be found in what the teacher talks about, and in the atmosphere surrounding the teaching event, but He should also be actively at work in the teacher himself or he as he presents the lesson. This must be a priority of every Pentecostal teacher. He must "eagerly desire" the operation of the Holy Spirit in his own teaching ministry (1 Cor. 12:31). I am reminded of the old African preacher who prayed, "Lord work *on* me, until you can work *in* me, until you can work *through* me." In all truly biblical teaching the teacher must be concerned with the

Holy Spirit working in and through him as he presents his lessons to his pupils.

In Jesus and the New Testament Teachers

Look again at the biblical model, and see how the Spirit flowed through Jesus and the teachers in the early church. Jesus testified concerning His own teaching that the words He spoke were not his own words but the words that the Father had given Him (John 8:28). He testified, "I did not speak of my own accord, but the Father who sent me commanded me what to say and how to say it" (12:49).

Jesus was declaring that the words which He spoke were not His own words, but came as a result of His relationship with the Father through the Holy Spirit. As He spoke and taught, the Spirit worked in Him revealing to Him the message of His Father. As a result of this flow of the Holy Spirit "the crowds were amazed at his teaching, because he taught as one who had authority, and not as their teachers of the law" (Matt. 7:28-29).

Paul exhorted Timothy, his son in the faith, "Do not neglect your gift, which was given you through the prophetic message when the body of elders laid hands on you" (1 Tim. 4:14). An examination of the context of Paul's statement reveals that the gift that was in Timothy was almost certainly the gift of teaching. Notice these phrases taken from the immediate context, all speaking of teaching:

- "things taught by demons" (v. 1)
- "instruct the brethren in these things" (v. 6, NKJV)
- "the good teaching that you followed" (v.6)
- "train yourself to be godly" (v. 7)
- "physical training" (v. 8)
- "command and teach these things (v. 11).

The Holy Spirit in the Presentation of Pentecostal Teaching

As with any spiritual gift, the gift of teaching can only be properly administered under the influence of the Holy Spirit. There must be a flow of the Holy Spirit as one teaches. Anything less is not true teaching in the New Testament sense.

In the Contemporary Pentecostal Teacher

Although teaching can be properly viewed as an activity of the intellect, for the Pentecostal teacher it must also be seen as an activity of the spirit. It is an anointing from God—His Spirit working in and through the spirit of the teacher. I am in no way trying to discourage proper training, preparation, and hard work. Such things are absolutely necessary for a successful teaching ministry. However, one must also understand that no amount of the above can produce an anointing from God resulting in a supernatural flow of spiritual life from the teacher to the student. Remember the words of Jesus, "The Spirit gives life; the flesh counts for nothing. The words I have spoken to you are spirit and they are life" (John 6:63).

Jesus was saying, "The words that I speak have their origin in the Spirit of God, and as a result they produce life in the lives of those who listen to them." There was a life-flow that came from His lips. This life-flow came as a result of His being anointed by the Spirit of the Lord (Luke 4:18-19). Paul said much the same thing about his teaching and preaching ministry: "My message [that is, my words] and my preaching were ... with a demonstration of the Spirit's power (1 Cor. 2:4). Whether preaching or teaching, Paul's very words were a demonstration of the Spirit's power and presence in his life.

As I have already stated in Chapter 3, teaching should be viewed as a charismatic event. When done properly, it is an outflow of the Spirit of God (John 7:37-38), and involves the manifestation of spiritual gifts. Spiritual gifts come as supernatural anointings from the Spirit of God and are released by acts of faith on the part of the Spirit-filled teacher.

The operation of the gift of teaching, properly done, requires the same anointing as any other gift of the Spirit, whether it be the gift of tongues, or prophecy, or working of miracles. In fact, prophecy is itself an appropriate function of a truly biblical teaching ministry. Paul taught that the Holy Spirit often anoints the prophet "to instruct others" (1 Cor. 14:19).

Again, what we are calling for here is a Pentecostal, that is, a true New-Testament teaching model. If our teaching is to be truly Pentecostal, it must be more than the mere passing on of information, even information about the Holy Spirit. It must be, rather, the transfer of spiritual dynamic. Like Peter and John, the Pentecostal teacher must be able to say to his or her students, "What I do have I give you" (Acts 3:6). And what he or she must have is a divine issue of the Holy Spirit flowing out of their innermost being (John 7:38),

The Holy Spirit's Role in Teaching

An important question naturally arises at this point in our discussion: If the Holy Spirit is to be involved in the presentation of truly Pentecostal teaching, how is this involvement to take place? The Holy Spirit should be actively involved in our teaching in at least three ways:

First, there should be a constant "inflow" into the life and spirit of the teacher. As he prepares and teaches his lessons the Pentecostal teacher does so under a dynamic inflow of the Holy Spirit. In Pentecostal circles we have traditionally called this inflow of the Spirit the anointing. We are speaking of the active and experienced presence of the Holy Spirit on and in the life of the teacher. When we say that the teacher should teach with anointing, we are saying that he should be presently and actively being filled with the Spirit as he teaches. He should be moving under the Spirit's guidance and prompting.

Such an anointing can only flow into, and thus out from, a life of consistent, abiding prayer. You will remember that, in Chapter 3, we noted that the context of Jesus' teaching was a powerful anointing with the Holy Spirit: "Now it happened on a certain day, as He was teaching ... the power of the Lord was present to heal them" (Luke 5:17).

From where did such anointing originate? The answer is found in the preceding verse: "Jesus often withdrew to lonely places and prayed" (v. 16). It was through His life of prayer that Jesus was constantly replenishing the river of the Spirit that flowed out of His being to touch others. If we are to have the same anointing as Jesus, then we must pay the same price—the price of a faithful and devoted prayer life.

By both word and example Jesus taught us that public blessing comes from private prayer. If we will spend time with God in the "secret place" our Father will reward us openly (Matt. 6:6). What greater reward can come to the teacher than the touch of the Spirit of God on his ministry?

This inflow of the Spirit into the heart of the teacher will often result in the manifestation of revelatory gifts of the Spirit, including words of knowledge and wisdom (1 Cor. 12:8-10). The needs of his students will be revealed to him, as well as divine answers to those needs. He will be given Spirit-inspired insight into the meaning and application of Scripture.

Secondly, along with constant inflow of the Spirit into the life of the teacher, there must also be a continual "outflow" of the same. Remember Jesus said that rivers of living water will flow *out of* our hearts (John 7:38). The teacher is not only to receive an anointing from the Holy Spirit, he is to pass it on to his students (1 Tim. 4:14). As words of knowledge and wisdom are given, the

Pentecostal teacher must speak them in faith. When prompted to speak a prophetic word, the teacher must speak out in faith. He must, at times, become a channel through which the Spirit speaks directly to his student. As the teacher speaks under such an anointing, his listeners will find themselves "quite unable to stand up against either his practical wisdom or the spiritual force with which he [speaks]" (Acts 6:10, Phillips). And as the teacher yields himself to the Spirit of God, he will find himself, like Paul and Barnabas, speaking "so effectively that great numbers [of people will believe]" (Acts 14:1).

The Pentecostal teacher's task involves more than the transfer of divine truth, in also involves the impartation of spiritual dynamic. As his students sit under his anointed teaching, there is an impartation of spiritual gifts into their own lives and ministries. His burden for the lost becomes their burden; his vision for ministry becomes their vision. As a result, they become like their teacher both in knowledge and in spirit.

Finally, as the Pentecostal teacher presents his lessons, there should be a demonstration of the Spirit's presence and power. If his students are to go out and minister in the power and anointing of the Holy Spirit, they must learn these things from their teacher. The secret of the apostles' power was not only their infilling with the Holy Spirit on the day of Pentecost, it was also their three and one half years of sitting at the feet of their anointed Teacher. It is the job of the Pentecostal teacher to model charismatic ministry to his students. He must in faith yield himself to the Spirit of God. He must allow the Holy Spirit to effect the release of spiritual gifts in his own life and ministry in order that his students might observe first hand a truly Pentecostal model for ministry.

Such modeling of charismatic ministry must take place both in class and out of class. It is the responsibility of the Pentecostal teacher to be an example of truly charismatic ministry to his students. Jesus said, "Everyone who is fully trained will be like his teacher" (Luke 6:40). Spirit-filled pastors will be produced only by Spirit-filled Bible school teachers.

Our Response

As we close this study on the Holy Spirit and teaching, I ask a final question: "What must we, as Pentecostal teachers, do in response to the powerful biblical truths which we have learned?" My answer is fourfold:

First, we must acknowledge the great importance of the implementation of a truly Pentecostal teaching model into our Bible schools and into our own teaching ministries. As Bible school administrators and teachers, our God-given assignment is to train an army of Spirit-anointed pastors, evangelists, teachers, and missionaries who will, in the power of the Holy Spirit, take the gospel to the yet-to-be-unreached peoples of the world. Such a powerful army can only be trained by those who are themselves truly Spirit-empowered.

Secondly, in order to accomplish our God-given task, we must seek greater understanding concerning the role and work of the Holy Spirit in our own teaching ministries. We must become students of the Spirit. We must never assume that we know all there is to know about life and ministry in the Spirit. We must rather commit ourselves anew to learn and relearn these things.

Third, we must seek to strengthen our relationship with the Spirit of God. Before we can ever see an outflow of spiritual life and spiritual gifts in our teaching ministries, there must first be an inflow of the Spirit's power and presence. We must, therefore, dedicate ourselves to a life of prayer in the Spirit. It must become a priority in our lives to learn to walk in daily fellowship with the Spirit of God. If we are going to keep on receiving from the Spirit, then we must "keep on asking ... seeking ... [and] knocking" (Luke 11:9).

And finally, if we are to truly fulfill our role as Pentecostal teachers, we must learn to walk and move in the power and anointing of the Holy Spirit. It is not enough to be able to name the nine spiritual gifts of 1Corinthians 12:8-10. Neither is it enough that we be able to define and catagorize them. No amount of head knowledge, however great, will suffice. We must be able to hear the voice of the Spirit, and in faith be able to move in the gifts of the Spirit. If we are to train truly Spirit-led ministers we must know how to follow the guidance of the Spirit ourselves. If we are to train truly Spirit-empowered ministers, we must ourselves know how to move in the power and gifts of the Holy Spirit. Having done these things maybe we can then say, "We are now teaching in the Spirit."

BIBLIOGRAPHY

Bonnke, Reinhard with George Canty. *Mighty Manifestations.* Eastbourne: Kingsway Publications, 1994.

Coleman, Robert, E. *The Master Plan of Evangelism.* Old Tappan, NJ: Fleming H. Revell Co., 1987.

Fee, Gordon. "Pauline Literature" in *Dictionary of Pentecostal and Charismatic Movements,* Stanley M. Burgess and Gary B. McGee, eds. Grand Rapids, MI: Zondervan Publishing House, 1988.

Gee, Donald. *The Gifts of the Spirit in the Working of the Ministry Today.* Springfield, MO: Gospel Publishing House, 1963.

Harris, Ralph W. *Complete Biblical Library, The New Testament Study Bible: Galatians—Philemon.* Springfield, MO: World Library Press, Inc., 1991.

Kuzmic, Peter. "Kingdom of God" in *Dictionary of Pentecostal and Charismatic Movements,* Stanley M. Burgess and Gary B. McGee, eds. Grand Rapids, MI: Zondervan Publishing House, 1988.

Menzies, William W. *Anointed to Serve.* Springfield, MO: Gospel Publishing House, 1971.

Wilson, Lewis F. "Bible Institutes, Colleges, Universities" in *Dictionary of Pentecostal and Charismatic Movements,* Stanley M. Burgess and Gary B. McGee, eds. Grand Rapids, MI: Zondervan Publishing House, 1988.

Other Books by the Author

Power Ministry: How to Minister in the Spirit's Power (2004)
(also available in French, Portuguese, Malagasy,
Kinyarwanda, and Chichewa)

*Empowered for Global Mission: A Missionary Look at
the Book of Acts* (2005)

From Azusa to Africa to the Nations (2005)
(also available in French, Spanish, and Portuguese)

Acts: The Spirit of God in Mission (2007)

In Step with the Spirit: Studies in the Spirit-filled Walk (2008)

*The Kingdom and the Power: The Kingdom of God:
A Pentecostal Interpretation* (2009)

*Experiencing the Spirit: A Study of the Work of the Spirit
in the Life of the Believer* (2009)

Teaching in the Spirit (2009)

*Power Encounter: Ministering in the Power and
Anointing of the Holy Spirit: Revised* (2009)
(also available in Kiswahili)

*You Can Minister in God's Power: A Guide for
Spirit-filled Disciples* (2009)

*The Spirit of God in Mission: A Vocational Commentary
on the Book of Acts* (2011)

Proclaiming Pentecost: 100 Sermon Outlines on the

Bibliography

Power of the Holy Spirit (2011)
(Available in French, Spanish, Portuguese, and Swahili)
(Associate editor with Mark Turney, editor)

Globalizing Pentecostal Missions in Africa (2011)
(Editor, with Enson Lwesya)

The 1:8 Promise of Jesus: The Key to World Harvest
(2012)

All of the above books are available from the
PneumaLife Publications
3766 N. Delaware Avenue
Springfield, MO, 65803, USA

E-mail: denny.miller@agmd.org

www.ingramcontent.com/pod-product-compliance
Lightning Source LLC
Chambersburg PA
CBHW060704030426
42337CB00017B/2757